Original title:

Searching for Meaning in All the Right Places

Author: Ronan Whitfield

ISBN HARDBACK: 978-1-80566-221-1

ISBN PAPERBACK: 978-1-80566-516-8

Embracing the Journey of Wonder

In a world full of maps, I lost my way,
Chasing squirrels down the street all day.
With a pocket full of dreams and socks askew,
I wonder if the sky is really that blue.

I peeked inside a toaster, looking for toast,
Found a lonely crumb that I'll cherish the most.
The mysteries of life in a mug of hot brew,
Do cups whisper secrets, or is that just you?

I danced with the shadows, played chase with the sun,
Told the moon a joke, but it just wouldn't run.
If laughter's the answer, then what's the great quest?
Are we all just a punchline, in life's silly jest?

So I skip and I hop, with no care for the map,
In a world of odd wonders, I refuse to cap.
With a grin on my face and a heart full of cheer,
I'll find what I seek, or at least I'll get near.

Voices Carried on the Breeze

Whispers in the air, oh so spry,
Chasing laughter as clouds drift by.
Socks mismatched, a jester's delight,
The sun giggles, painting the night.

Wandering souls with silly hats,
Barking dogs, and some lazy cats.
Climbing trees with comic flair,
Patchy fields of truth to share.

Puzzles Left to Unravel

Jigsaw pieces fit so wrong,
Can't find the edge, just sing a song.
A cat in a box, where could it be?
Questions dance like it's all just free.

Putting together a breakfast plate,
Eggs and toast, but wait, it's late!
The milk's a puzzle that won't fit right,
Sipping smoothies while we take flight.

The Heart's Compass in Wild Places

A lost compass leads the way,
To laughter's trail and a bright bouquet.
With giggles found in unusual spots,
Finding joy in forgotten pots.

Timid hearts in a bustling crowd,
Skip with glee, they're feeling proud.
Like turtles in roller skates they glide,
In this merry dance, there's nowhere to hide.

Falling Leaves and Fateful Turns

Leaves tumble down, what a sight!
They giggle and swirl in autumn's light.
Each twist and turn, a quirky fate,
Laughter ripples, don't be late!

Grab a twig, make a wand,
With silly spells, of which we're fond.
Chasing shadows, we sometimes trip,
In this goofy world, let's find our grip.

Looking for Fragments of Light

In the fridge, I seek my muse,
A leftover pizza? I'd gladly choose.
Dancing in the glow of the screen,
Finding joy in crumbs of the cuisine.

My socks, they don't match, but who really cares?
I search for wisdom in tangled hair.
A sock drawer's depth, a puzzle so vast,
Who knew laundry could hold such a blast?

I check the garden for wild ideas,
Among the weeds, I confront my fears.
A flower blooms where I once saw mud,
Nature's way of showing me love!

The Sweetness of Wandering Hearts

A map's in my pocket, but I'm just a fool,
I'll follow the ice cream truck, that's my rule.
Sweet cones to chase, with sprinkles galore,
Wandering freely, I'll always want more.

Lost in the park, let's run with the ducks,
Every quack they make, is just pure luck.
With giggles and snacks, we'll conquer the day,
Who knew joy could lead us so far away?

Under the sun, we'll laugh and we'll sing,
Finding new joy in the simplest things.
Wandering hearts with no map in sight,
Making memories, oh what a delight!

Finding Serenity in Stillness

In my backyard, I sit really still,
A squirrel is plotting an epic thrill.
He snacks away while I sip my tea,
Moments like this are truly carefree.

The cat on the fence judges my life,
As if she's the queen and I'm the strife.
But I notice the buzz of the bee in flight,
Serenity wrapped in a warm sunlight.

The stillness hums an off-key song,
My mind discovers where I belong.
In the quiet chaos, I find my cheer,
Laughter and peace, they draw ever near.

The Colors That Shape Our Stories

Crayons out, let's start the chase,
Painting life with a goofy face.
Every splash a giggle, every stroke a glee,
Coloring outside? Oh, just let it be!

Purple skies where the green grass grows,
Can't find my shoes, oh well, who knows?
Maybe the sun will fit on my shoe,
As I aim for the best, but miss the cue.

In this canvas of other folks' dreams,
I'll paint a rainbow that gently beams.
Shape my tales with laughter and laughter's hue,
For every splash tells my story too!

Refractions of Truth in Clear Waters

In the mirror of the lake, I see,
A fish wearing glasses, staring back at me.
It's trying to decipher a hidden joke,
As I ponder why the snapper called me folk.

Sunbeams dance on the surface, so bright,
While ducks debate who's the best in flight.
With a splash, they quack their grand release,
I'm left wondering if I'll ever find peace.

Bubbles rise up with secrets untold,
I'm fishing for wisdom, not bait made of gold.
The water tells tales, a comedy spree,
Of turtles who claim they've set blobs of free.

In clear waters, the truth wears a mask,
While I search for answers—it's no simple task.
But laughter rings loud through the ripples' cheer,
In this liquid landscape, my vision is clear.

Moments of Clarity in the Storm

Raindrops tap dance on my windowpane,
As clouds share sarcasm, it's hard to complain.
Lightning flickers with a wink and a grin,
Thunder cracks jokes—will the fun ever thin?

Blown umbrellas become playful kites,
While puddles mirror my muddled delights.
I slip and I slide, a delightful ballet,
Each splash brings a chuckle, come join the fray!

The wind howls a tune, off-key but sincere,
I'm drumming my heart with a grin ear to ear.
Moments of clarity wrapped in a storm,
Reality's giggles begin to transform.

As the tempest rumbles, I find my own voice,
In the chaos around, I'm making a choice.
To dance in confusion, embrace the wild ride,
Where laughter meets chaos, and storms coincide.

Threads of Destiny Interwoven

In the tapestry of life, I see threads of glee,
Knots tied by my cat while I sip on my tea.
Each fray has a story, a flicker of fate,
As I ponder my purpose with a side of debate.

Woolen wafts whisper as I weave my way,
To snags of serendipity, come here, come play!
In the fabric of time, a patch might just fit,
With laughter the needle pokes yet avoids all the grit.

Each color that's spun tells a whimsical tale,
Of socks gone missing, lost on a trail.
A scarf tangled up in the twists of the night,
Yet somehow, through humor, it feels just right.

When the loom starts to chatter, I join in the fun,
For each loop and each weft bring the joy of a pun.
In threads of connection, my path's never lone—
I stitch a good story, no need for a throne.

The Quiet Pursuit of the Real

In the library of life, I tiptoe so slow,
While books tell tales of the things I don't know.
With each turned page, a riddle I find,
A chapter of chaos written in kind.

The shelves sigh and whisper, 'Did you check the vault?'
Where ideas of candy and dreams are exalted.
I stumble on wisdom, absurd and absurd,
While a librarian smirks at the thoughts I've stirred.

There's magic in moments when I drop the charade,
A secret revealed in a cupcake parade.
The frosting of truth swirls with a wink,
As I chase the absurd into thoughts that may sink.

With each quirky lesson, I giggle and reel,
As I wander through nonsense in search of the real.
In this quiet pursuit, where folly prevails,
I embrace the bizarre; it's a life full of tales.

The Echo of Intent in Silent Hours

In the quiet corners, the whispers play,
Where socks go missing, they laugh all day.
Intentions like echoes, they bounce around,
Yet clarity hides where no one has found.

With coffee cups stacked, a mountain of dreams,
I question my choices, or so it seems.
The clock ticks louder, a comedic clock,
Tick-tock goes wisdom, like a funny old rock.

A cat sneezes softly, I ponder my fate,
As crumbs from breakfast seem slightly too late.
Intentions are mice, scurrying with glee,
While laughter remains my best company.

In silent hours, I search yet deny,
The simple existence of pie in the sky.
So I toast to confusion, my heart in dismay,
With each silly thought that just waltzes away.

Where Footprints Lead to Discovery

With each step I take, the earth starts to spin,
Footprints of laughter, where do I begin?
A misstep on puddles launches me high,
Like a leap of decision, oh my, oh my.

The map in my pocket shows nothing at all,
Yet I venture forth like a wacky basketball.
Each mark tells a story, a dance of delight,
Where socks lost to mysteries are quite the sight.

I trip on a dream as it throws me around,
A tumble of wonders, where joy can be found.
Footprints unmatched, they tell silly tales,
With giggles of ghosts that float on the gales.

So here's to the journey and routes that amaze,
With paths that are tangled in whimsical ways.
In the end, all these footprints will guide,
To discoveries waiting, right there in my stride.

The Weight of Yearning and Hope

Yearning comes heavy, like a sack full of bricks,
Propped up by dreams and odd little tricks.
Hope dances like noodles fallen from stew,
Making meaning of moments, it wobbles askew.

A frown turns to laughter with a wink from the cat,
As I ponder my future in that silly old hat.
The weight can be daunting, like socks in a dryer,
Yet hope sprouts wings, a comical flyer.

With every odd tumble, my heart starts to hum,
Like a waltzing potato, a weird kind of drum.
Each yearn is a giggle, a silly parade,
Where the weight of it all slowly starts to fade.

So let's laugh at the weight and adjust our tall crown,
For hopes that seem heavy can flip upside down.
In the dance of absurdity, joy we'll ignite,
As we navigate this wacky, wild plight.

Illuminating the Shadows of Doubt

In the shadows of doubt, where giggles reside,
I dance with my sneakers, on emotions I slide.
The light casts strange shapes, like a puzzled old mime,
Doubt's just a jester, running out of time.

I chase after twinkles that wink in the gloom,
As doubts do the cha-cha, transforming the room.
With each silly stumble, I find a new path,
Where humor illuminates the aftermath.

An umbrella of laughter shields me from fear,
While shadows make shadows with jokes in their ear.
So I jive with the whispers that tickle my mind,
As the glow of absurdity is always kind.

Let's shine through the murk with a quirk and a jest,
Doubt can't outshine me, I'm wearing my best.
With laughter as armor, I waltz past the flaws,
Illuminating life with a funny applause.

In the Footsteps of Our Ancestors

We danced with ghosts in ancient shoes,
Their steps were silly, we couldn't refuse.
With giggles and jigs, our laughter soared,
Learning their tricks, we just couldn't be bored.

They showed us the way through fields of dreams,
Told us to follow the bright moonbeams.
With each funny tale and quirky rhyme,
We found our joy, soaking up the time.

The Hidden Symphony of Our Lives

Life's a concert, quite offbeat,
With cymbals clashing and tapping feet.
We waltzed with waffles, we cha-cha'd with cheese,
Instruments squeaked like a flock of bees.

Amidst the chaos, we played tunes so fine,
Harmonizing jokes and some cheap red wine.
Each note a giggle, each pause a laugh,
We composed a masterpiece—a wacky craft.

A Quest Beneath the Midnight Sky

Under the stars, we set out bold,
Chasing our dreams, or so we were told.
With map upside down, we wander and roam,
In search of treasure—where's our comfy home?

We tripped over twigs and giggled with glee,
Stumbling and tumbling, as lost as can be.
Yet in the moonlight, we found our flair,
For treasure's not gold, but joy in the air.

When Hearts Whisper in the Night

In the stillness, hearts start to chat,
Sharing sweet secrets while feeling quite fat.
They laugh and they sigh, a giggle or two,
Like chubby little cherubs, all decked out in blue.

With starlight above, and shadows that creep,
Hearts debate cookies, and dreams on a heap.
In the hush of the night, they find what they crave,
Together they dance, and misbehave!

Journeys Within an Infinite Sky

Up in the clouds, where lost socks hide,
I ponder the secrets that joy can't confide.
Is it the fondue of life or just cheese?
Navigating nonsense with a pinch of ease.

Astronauts rocket, while I float in my chair,
Chasing bold dreams that lead to nowhere.
A flight of fancy, a wild goose chase,
Falling for puddles yet dancing with grace.

The Silent Murmurs of the Soul

My heart whispers tales of pasta and pies,
In the quietest moments, it still tries.
What's the purpose of shoes that don't fit?
Do they teach me to ice skate or just sit?

With laughter as my compass, I sail through the day,
Listening closely as the world has its say.
A riddle wrapped up in laughter's sweet song,
Who knew the dance of life could be so wrong?

In the Ruins of Yesterday

Yesterday's worries, like crumbs in a dish,
Make me ponder where dreams go to swish.
Is it the cat that knows more than me?
Or is it the cactus that holds the key?

Among the ruins, I stumble and trip,
Over mismatched socks and the occasional nip.
A quest to recover the lost and the fun,
Digging for treasures under the sun.

A Dance with Fleeting Moments

In the dance of the seconds, I twirl with delight,
Chasing down time as if it were a kite.
Each tick's a tickle, a giggle, a grin,
Ticklish moments where joys begin.

Fleeting flashes, like fireflies at dusk,
Remind me to savor the chaos, not rush.
With every misstep, a chuckle occurs,
As I reel with the woes of the world and its slurs.

The Unspoken Language of the Universe

Stars wink like cheeky stars,
Whispers in a cosmic breeze.
Gravity just wants to pull,
While we dance, we must appease.

Galaxies spin their old tales,
Black holes with a playful grin.
Einstein had it figured out,
But forgot to factor in gin.

Planets gossip in their orbits,
Asteroids throw shade like pros.
Comets are just flashy trends,
And meteors? Just rock stars' shows.

So grab your telescope, my friend,
And listen closely to the night.
For in the silence of the dark,
Laughter sings, oh what a sight!

Notes from an Unwritten Journey

Packed my bags with socks and dreams,
Found a map that had no lines.
Paved roads lead to spicy schemes,
Detours stocked with colorful signs.

One wrong turn, a joyful laugh,
Met a llama who wore a hat.
We exchanged our best life tips,
She said, "You talk to cats, how 'bout that?"

Chasing sunsets on a tricycle,
Pedals squeak, I feel alive.
Every twist, a new to-do,
Who needs plans? Let's just dive!

At the end, we found our path,
In a bowl of noodles deep.
Life's a guidebook full of laughs,
Let's ripple in joy, not leap!

The Dance of Questions in Twilight

Why does daylight take a bow?
Is it all a cosmic trick?
Moonlight giggles, stars say wow,
As shadows dance a moonlit flick.

What if clouds were just lost sheep?
Why do crickets serenade?
With every twinkle, laughter cheap,
Seriousness? Just a charade.

Why does the wind like to tease?
Could it be a lover's game?
Leaves respond with flirty ease,
Tree trunks blush, it's quite the fame.

So twirl with questions in the air,
With each giggle, find your glee.
For in the twilight, everywhere,
Lies a hint of mystery!

Unseen Paths of Connection

Two socks in the dryer, they flee,
Choosing freedom, no plain view.
Is there a sock-party spree?
Maybe they're just tired of you!

Coffee mugs that cheer each day,
Whispering secret brew delights.
What do microwaves really say?
They hum their love, into the nights.

Cats muse over life and fate,
Paws pressed close to dusty screens.
What do they contemplate?
More naps, or are they plotting schemes?

So let us wander, hand in hand,
In mismatched shoes, we'll make our way.
For through each quirky twist, we'll stand,
And laugh as night turns into day!

The Secret in the Rustle of Leaves

In the park where the squirrels dart,
I hear whispers that tickle my heart.
A breeze dances, so cool and spry,
Telling secrets where the shadows lie.

The pigeons argue, a feathery debate,
While I ponder my lunch on a plate.
Are they wise, or just taking a break?
I'll follow them—let's see what they make!

The leaves giggle as they swirl around,
"What's the meaning?" is what I have found.
With every rustle, a joke they share,
I laugh out loud; do they even care?

So I sit with my thoughts and a slice of pie,
Life's funny moments softly drift by.
I'll take the giggles, leave worries behind,
For joy hides in places we often can't find.

A Journey Through the Labyrinth of Self

In a maze made of thoughts, I wander without route,
Where mirrors reflect a playful doubt.
I meet my twin, who's a bit of a clown,
He giggles and whispers, "Don't wear that frown!"

With every turn, I discover some cheese,
The kind that smells like forgotten old knees.
If I get lost, I'll dance with the walls,
Who needs directions? Let's have ourselves a ball!

Through winding paths that twist and twirl,
I spot my hopes in this hilarious whirl.
Each step I take, I'm tripping on dreams,
Laughing at life's silly, tangled seams.

So here's to the journey, as goofy as jest,
Finding my way was a humorous quest.
With every wrong turn, I grin ear to ear,
For the maze is much brighter when you laugh out of fear!

Finding Clarity in the Chaotic

In a world where confusion reigns supreme,
I juggle my thoughts like a wild circus dream.
The clock ticks loudly; it's quite the chime,
While I sip my coffee, pondering rhyme.

The cat on the couch looks wise and old,
With secrets untold in her fur of gold.
I ask her for help; she yawns with a sigh,
"Why bother, dear friend? Just let chaos fly!"

Amid swirling papers and crumbs on my plate,
I spot a solution that's frankly first-rate.
It's hiding in laughter, a tickle of grace,
Wrapped snug in the chaos, it finds its own place.

So I'll dance with the clutter, embrace the unknown,
For clarity flows when the wild seeds are sown.
A chuckle, a wiggle, a wink in the fray,
Brings joy to the mess, in a wobbly way!

Beneath the Surface of Everyday Life

Amid the hustle, the bustle, the rush,
I search for the humor in every small crush.
The toast that burns, the socks that don't pair,
Even the cat who gives me a stare.

At the store, I'm lost in the maze of the aisles,
Fruits whisper stories, and veggies have smiles.
The cereal struts in its colorful coat,
Winking at me like it's ready to float.

The coffee shop hums with laughter and cheer,
Each sip a reminder that joy is quite near.
The barista's jokes bubble up like the brew,
And I leave with a grin, feeling fresh and anew.

So here's to the layers we peel back each day,
With giggles and quirks mixed in the display.
For underneath life's pressures and strife,
Lies a treasure of laughter—oh, what a life!

Songs of the Uncharted

In the fridge, I hear a tune,
A dancing carrot and a spoon.
In closet shadows, laughter grows,
A sock that's lost, but nobody knows.

Mice on bicycles ride the floor,
While dust bunnies open a door.
With every creak, the house joins in,
A concert hall where chaos wins.

Chairs tell tales of late-night snacks,
And cats perform their stealthy hacks.
Under the bed, a monster hums,
But I just laugh; it's probably dumb.

So join the chorus, sing along,
With socks and spoons, where we belong.
Embrace the chaos, let it flow,
In this wild show, we steal the show.

In Pursuit of Silent Truths

Under the sink, a rubber duck,
Holds secrets low, just pure luck.
The plants conspire, they take their stand,
Whispering hints with leafy hands.

In the backyard, gnomes hold court,
Debating which way the squirrels ought.
The fence eavesdrops on their grand schemes,
While I just watch, lost in my dreams.

The cat's a sage with mystical views,
As it ponders life in puddles of dew.
A world of wonders just out of sight,
A riddle wrapped in a feline bite.

So follow the path where oddities meet,
In this realm of giggles, life's not so sweet.
Here lies the fun, in the quirks we find,
The silent truths that tickle the mind.

Stars Behind Closed Eyes

In the mind, a circus plays,
With elephants dancing in sunlit rays.
Cotton candy clouds float on by,
As dreams take flight, oh my, oh my!

Jellybean stars twinkling bright,
Tickle the fancies of the night.
Underneath blankets, silly worlds spin,
Where giggles are currency, let the fun begin.

A grand parade of thoughts afloat,
Riding on dreams like a silly boat.
Teddies compete in a pancake race,
In the kitchen, there's no need for grace.

So snuggle in tight, let whimsy reign,
Where laughter bursts like a soda's refrain.
Behind closed eyes, adventure ignites,
With stars that sparkle and fanciful flights.

The Alchemy of Wonder

In the backyard, herbs hold a chat,
About the latest gossip and all of that.
Tomatoes critique the weather each day,
While carrots roll their eyes at the play.

A funny wizard with a mop for a hat,
Spells silly potions; don't you dare sat!
A dash of giggles, a pinch of delight,
Stirring up magic that's sure to excite.

Cakes made of clouds and candy rain,
Turn frowns upside down, release all the pain.
In this kitchen of joy, nothing's too strange,
Mixing absurd with a little bit of change.

So gather around for a taste of the fun,
Life's a big kitchen, with humor to run.
We'll bake up our dreams in ridiculous ways,
Creating a feast of the silliest days.

The Fabric of Hopes and Fears

In a closet full of dreams, I dive,
Tangled sweaters, where wishes thrive.
A sock with secrets, a shirt with glee,
All of them wait, to set my mind free.

I measure my thoughts with a tape of yarn,
Crafting my plans without a warn.
With needles of giggles, I stitch my strife,
Unraveling chaos, I knit up my life.

Currents of the Mind's River

Floating down the stream of thought,
I paddle with paddles that I forgot.
A rubber duck quacks out some advice,
As fish in bow ties offer me rice.

With marshmallow clouds drifting above,
I bottle up giggles, fill it with love.
The current pulls, but I steer quite wide,
Oars made of laughter help me glide.

Whispers Through the Void

Echoes of giggles in the empty air,
I decode their secrets, don't have a care.
A taco with wings flies by with flair,
Chasing around dreams with a leap and a scare.

The silence buzzes with playful delight,
As shadows play peek-a-boo in the night.
I wave at my worries, they stumble away,
In this void of whispers, I dance and sway.

The Quest Beneath the Stars

Under the blanket of twinkling lights,
I search for answers, not just for sights.
A shooting star trips over a wish,
While aliens giggle, serving up fish.

My compass spins in a cosmic swirl,
While meteors waltz and comets twirl.
I trudge on paths of luminous dust,
With silly cosmic hat on, I must!

Echoes of an Unseen Path

In a cupboard full of maps, I found,
A treasure chest of socks, quite profound.
With crumbs of wisdom underneath,
I laughed at fate's quirky wreath.

Beneath a couch where I misplaced dreams,
I found more dust than glittering gleams.
Each hidden nook held forgotten clues,
To mysteries wrapped in old, worn shoes.

The garden gnome winked, shared a tale,
Of quirky paths and a three-legged snail.
As roosters crowed their own sweet song,
I pondered where the lost socks belong.

The moon giggled from her cozy chair,
With secrets of life swirling everywhere.
As I marched on with my mismatched feet,
The path unwound in a dance so sweet.

In the Embrace of Forgotten Dreams

Once chased by a cloud with a fluffy face,
I stumbled upon a banana peel's grace.
In the embrace of dreams tucked tight,
I cracked up at a snail's snail-like flight.

A tree whispered of wishes in the breeze,
Of forgotten things, like a child's lost keys.
Each twinkling star was a wink in disguise,
As I conversed with a very wise fly.

With laughter echoing in soda cans,
I discovered the truth beneath playful plans.
Tickling my fancy with a spaghetti stare,
I dived into life without a care.

So I danced with shadows and played with delight,
Finding humor in day and levity in night.
In this laugh-filled quest, I came to find,
The beauty in chaos, joy intertwined.

Threads of Time and Purpose

I spun a yarn with a curious cat,
Who claimed to know where all the cheese sat.
Every tangled thread made me trip,
As I stumbled through this colorful blip.

Old clocks chuckled with their ticking chime,
Saying, "You're late to the party, old time!"
I danced with moments that giggled and spun,
While counting my blessings, I forgot to run.

A bridge made of fettuccine swayed,
As I wove through dreams, not afraid.
With each step, I tasted the sauce of fate,
Wondering if I'd ever get straight.

So let's toast to the quirks of our race,
With laughter and noodles, we'll find our place.
In the tapestry of life, so absurd and grand,
We've got threads of purpose knit by hand.

The Light Beyond the Horizon

I followed a light that flickered and danced,
In a sock drawer, that old romance.
It giggled and twinkled, leading me near,
To the golden glow of a pint of beer.

The sun wore shades, quite a sight to behold,
As I chased shadows, feeling quite bold.
Laughter erupted from the trees' leafy mouth,
Echoing secrets from the south.

Fish in a pond had a stand-up show,
While squirrels exchanged what they didn't know.
With my heart full of chuckles, I strolled with glee,
Through this circus of life, just being free.

So here's to the light that doesn't make sense,
To the punchlines that live in our nonsense.
With every twist and turn that life provides,
We'll keep laughing on this wild, crazy ride.

The Artisan of Dreams

In a workshop of hopes, I craft my delight,
With yarns of butterflies, and wishes in flight.
I'm stitching together my ambitions with flair,
But the thread's gone missing—oh, where's my spare?

With paintbrush and palette, I'll draw a new face,
A giggling giraffe on rollers, a race!
Yet every time I step back to inspect,
I find that my canvas has gone to collect.

So I'm weaving a tapestry, bright as the day,
With unicorns prancing in a fanciful way.
But who knew that glitter could make such a mess?
My workshop now looks like a festive distress!

Yet laughter erupts in this glorious quest,
For each little blunder becomes a grand jest.
As I shake off the chaos, smiles in each seam,
I'm crafting a life that's a whimsical dream.

Discovering Sunlight's Embrace

I stood on the sidewalk, not quite sure I'd go,
But the sun had that twinkle, that cheeky glow.
In search of adventure, I donned my bright shades,
And stepped into laughter where shadows cascades.

The trees danced with whispers, leaves tickling air,
While squirrels debated their midday affair.
I tripped over daisies, their heads held up high,
As they chuckled aloud—oh my, oh my!

With each step I took, there were giggles galore,
The pigeons were squawking—were they keeping score?
I found that the journey was funny, you see,
In sunlight's embrace, I felt totally free.

So I twirled 'neath the rays, like a ballerina,
With shades still intact and a funky subpoena.
This quest for delight makes the silliest song,
Finding joy in each moment, where I truly belong.

The Heart's Hidden Atlas

With maps made of muffins and compasses sweet,
I set off to find where my heart longs to greet.
Each crumb is a landmark, each frosting a guide,
But I'm lost in this pastry—oh, what do I hide?

The cupcakes conspire, they giggle and bounce,
As I wander through sprinkles, a sugary flounce.
And every wrong turn leads to laughter galore,
When I trip on a brownie and tumble on floor.

In this galaxy swirling with candy and pie,
I followed a chocolate chip star in the sky.
But instead of solutions, I found a white booth,
Where cake slices giggled—oh, that's the truth!

So I toast with my juice of a thousand fruit dreams,
With laughed-out adventures that burst at the seams.
In my heart's hidden atlas, I finally see,
That the map was the journey, the sweetest of glee.

Fragments of a Wandering Mind

Oh, my brain is a puzzle of mismatched pieces,
With socks on the loose and my thought train increases.
I'm hunting for treasures in a storm of confetti,
Where echoes of giggles haunt corners quite petty.

I jotted down wisdom on napkins and walls,
But each time I blinked, I'd forget what befalls.
So I scribble and doodle till art starts to leap,
While rubber band thoughts perform tricks that are deep.

With thoughts weaving tales like a cat in a yarn,
I chase after ideas that twinkle and brawn.
Yet laughter erupts when a punchline goes shy,
As a chipmunk named Cedric zooms past in the sky.

So I wander this maze of nonsense and cheer,
With joy in my heart and my mind without fear.
For each little fragment that juggles my time,
Becomes part of my journey, my very own rhyme.

When the Earth Speaks

The rocks tumble tales so absurd,
With gossiping trees, whispers unheard.
A squirrel in a suit, quite the charmer,
Debates with a mole, quite the farmer.

Clouds have opinions on the weather,
While ants carry crumbs, light as a feather.
A snail with a monocle reads the flow,
In the land of giggles, where secrets grow.

Layers of Light and Shadow

A shadow plays hide-and-seek with the sun,
As giggles erupt, oh what fun!
The light will tickle, the dark will play,
Dancing through moments, come join the fray.

Behind the curtain, the mischief brews,
With the moon sneaking peeks, sharing news.
With shadows casting goofy shapes,
A game of laughter and silly tapes.

The Garden of Forgotten Dreams

In the garden where lost thoughts bloom,
A dandelion wears a wizard's costume.
The daisies gossip, petals all aflutter,
While butterflies laugh, playing in the clutter.

A whimsical breeze whispers old schemes,
Tickling the nose of sleep-laden dreams.
Every weed has a story to spin,
In this garden of giggles, let joy begin.

Unveiling the Invisible

Behind every door, a joke waits to fly,
Invisible puppets dance in the sky.
The tickles of laughter, just out of sight,
While rainbows argue what colors are right.

Ghosts of humor float, oh so free,
With giggles that echo, come join the spree.
In every corner, a chuckle's confined,
Unveiling the silly, oh what a find!

The Odyssey of Everyday Moments

In a grocery aisle, I ponder life,
Should I buy kale or a slice of pie?
Adventure calls in the cereal maze,
But it's just me and my shopping cart spy.

Lost in a maze of choices galore,
Each label whispers, "Pick me, pick me!"
Pasta or rice? Oops, I dropped a can,
This quest for tacos ends in a spree.

At the checkout, I stand wide-eyed,
Fruits or snacks? I can't decide!
A store clerk laughs, she knows my plight,
Saying, "Join my club, it's a fun ride!"

Outside the store, the sun shines bright,
I juggle bags, a circus in flight.
Every moment's a treasure, silly and sweet,
Today with snacks, tomorrow with light.

Reaching for Stars from Grounded Roots

With toes in the grass, I gaze at the sky,
Wishing for rockets, but here comes a bee.
My dreams take flight on a picnic blanket,
Here's a sandwich!¿Please don't buzz around me?

A star shines bright, in my lunchbox, lost,
Tuna? Or chicken? The choice is a whirl.
I toss a few chips to enhance my luck,
But I just feed the ants who dance in a twirl.

Gather round friends with their tales on the breeze,
Each fable takes off, like kites in a race.
But secretly, we're just eating pizza,
Reaching for dreams, one bite in our case.

When night falls, we build a star chart in hand,
Pointing to constellations in silence we stand.
Yet the best part of all is the laughter we share,
Grounded in moments, life's funniest brand.

Searching Through the Sands of Time

With a cup of coffee, I ponder my fate,
Should I be a wizard or just a dull mate?
I scroll through my phone, each scroll takes a while,
And here comes my cat with a self-satisfied smile.

In the sandbox of life, I buried my toys,
Lost in the trenches, yet making some noise.
A sand timer spins, telling tales of the past,
How did I end up with a hat that won't last?

As the grains slide slowly, I stumble on gold,
But it's just some old snacks, what a story they told!
Time's a magician, and I am its fool,
Eating stale chips while I stand near a pool.

Each hour that passes, I laugh and I sigh,
Time seems to melt faster than a pie in July.
But despite the chaos, I find joy in the sand,
In the mess and the moments, life's perfectly planned.

Mysteries Enfolded in the Ordinary

Each morning unfolds with a toast in my hand,
How does bread give rise to such fluff? Isn't it grand?
Should I spread peanut butter or this jelly so bold?
The mysteries multiply before they grow cold.

The sidewalk cracks hold secrets, do you hear?
A lost penny whispers of fortune and cheer.
But I just step over, with a snack in my pocket,
Savoring moments like a chef with a locket.

Upside down rainbows, they float by my side,
As I chase caffeine dreams on my bicycle ride.
I may find a unicorn under that tree,
But it's just a squirrel who seems happy and free.

So here in the mundane, I find endless delight,
Pursuing the mysteries found every night.
Life is a puzzle, with parts that are funny,
In the ordinary magic, I shine like a honey.

A Heartbeat Echoing Through Time

In the fridge, I find my muse,
A week-old pizza, oh, what a ruse!
Each slice whispers tales long gone,
Of midnight snacks and friendship's song.

I chase the cat, it runs away,
Is it meaning, or just play?
With every pounce, my mind takes flight,
Is this profound or just delight?

The clock ticks loud, a sneaky tease,
Is it wisdom, or just cheese?
Each heartbeat echoes, thumps in rhyme,
As I ponder snacks at half past nine.

So come with me, and let's explore,
The quirky life behind each door!
For in these giggles, laughter shines,
As we fetch the truth from silly signs.

Unlocking Doors of Perception

I rummaged through my tangled thoughts,
Found a sock, but what it taught!
A mystery wrapped in a fuzzy tale,
Of laundry days and epic fail.

I knocked on doors pretending hush,
A pizza man? Or genius rush?
With every promise of tasty pie,
I realized I'm just a guy.

Peeking through the keyhole's eye,
A world of laughter, oh so nigh.
Unlocking dreams, a playful scheme,
Is this life or just a meme?

Each door a chance, each step a dance,
In this madcap world, take a chance!
With joy and whimsy as my guide,
I'll find the truth where fun resides.

Where Love Meets the Horizon

A horizon blushes, gold and pink,
Where love and pizza intersect, I think!
With cheesy lines that stretch so wide,
We laugh at the moon, oh what a ride!

In a field of socks, I find my heart,
Each lost one plays a crucial part.
My feelings rise like dough in heat,
I guess that's how love tastes so sweet!

As owls hoot and stars twinkle bright,
We ponder life in soft moonlight.
With every giggle that we share,
We unearth meaning from midair.

So hold my hand, let's trek this path,
Through silliness and joyous math!
For where love goes, we surely roam,
On this zany quest, we create our home.

The Light That Breaks the Darkness

In the fridge, a light shines bright,
A leftover cake, oh what a sight!
With every slice, the shadows flee,
One bite reveals the mystery!

The dishes stack like wisdom tall,
But in this chaos, here's the ball!
I twirl and dance, much to the glee,
The light that breaks is cake and me.

As socks unite in vibrant pairs,
I ponder life, despite the snares.
In every giggle, joy ignites,
Where laughter blooms, there's hope in sights.

So raise a toast to silly quests,
In every mishap, joy invests!
For with each chuckle, darkness dips,
We find our spark, in quirky trips.

Unraveling the Tapestry of Existence

In the closet, I found a sock,
It told me jokes and danced like a clock.
My cat rolled her eyes, unimpressed,
While I searched for truth in the mess.

The fridge hummed a curious tune,
As I pondered life with a plastic spoon.
The leftovers giggled, begging for fate,
But I chose the cereal—my breakfast date.

Outside, the birds wore tiny hats,
While I tried to chat with the neighborhood rats.
They rolled their eyes as if to say,
"It's just another zany Thursday!"

Life's a riddle, a game gone sore,
Where answers hide behind every door.
Yet I chase the laughter on the breeze,
Unraveling threads, doing what I please.

Chasing Shadows of the Heart

I spilled my thoughts on a café table,
Sipping my coffee, feeling quite able.
The barista winked, told a quirky tale,
Of love found in socks, instead of a gale.

My heart's a balloon, it floats and bobs,
Tangled in thoughts, just like my jobs.
Yet I giggle along with a slice of pie,
Finding joy in dessert, oh me, oh my!

The garden whispers with bees aplenty,
And each flower giggles, oh so dainty.
As I chase shadows buzzing in glee,
They point and laugh, hearts wild and free.

So I dance through life with a grin so wide,
With each silly stumble, my heart's my guide.
Chasing these shadows that play hide and seek,
Turns out the punchline is quite unique!

The Map of Lost Intentions

In a drawer, I found a crumpled map,
Promised treasure, but turned into scrap.
X marked the spot where I lost my keys,
And then I tripped on the cat with a sneeze.

With each step, my plans seem to wander,
Like a confused sheep, I scratch my ponder.
The compass spins like a carnival ride,
As I search for sense with a coffee beside.

My thoughts are like bubbles, they float and pop,
Each idea's a noodle, I can't find the shop.
Yet laughter bubbles up, sweet and bright,
As I chase paper boats in the moonlight.

In the end, it's a whimsical quest,
Finding joy in the chaos, feeling blessed.
The map may be lost, but who needs a plan?
With giggles and mishaps, I've truly begun.

Waves of Thought on Silent Shores

At the beach, I carved my dreams in sand,
But the waves ran up and said, "Not so grand!"
They giggled along as I chased the tide,
Socks all wet, with a seagull as guide.

With each wave, my worries washed away,
And I asked a clam, "What do you say?"
It closed its shell, ignoring my plea,
While I sketched my plans, remarkably free!

The sun was a helper, painting the sky,
While I tried to understand, but thought, "Oh my!"
The tides rolled in, with laughter so bright,
Seashells chimed in, "You'll be alright!"

So I danced on the shore, barefooted and bold,
Building castles of dreams, vivid and gold.
With waves of thought, I leap and I soar,
Finding joy in the silliness evermore!

Whispers of the Unseen

In the corners of my mind's vast land,
A sock whispers secrets, so unplanned.
It claims it's hiding, not lost at all,
Just avoiding my laundry's loud call.

A cat in the window looks quite wise,
With a twitch of its tail, it starts to advise.
"Chase that red dot, it must hold a clue,
Or just forget it and nap like I do."

Behind the fridge, a meeting's held,
Where crumbs and dust bunnies have rebelled.
They plot their escape under fruit bowls,
Declaring freedom, while I scroll on my goals.

Yet amidst the chaos and the stray toys,
I stumble upon unexpected joys.
A rubber duck, a forgotten smile,
In life's joke, I've lingered a while.

The Quest Beyond the Horizon

A fortune cookie claimed I'd find gold,
But all I've got is this tale that's old.
From couch cushions, I hope to extract,
The treasure of snacks that I've long lost track.

With a map made of crumbs and a heart full of glee,
I voyage to the fridge, oh, what will it be?
A quest for leftovers, fresh or moldy,
This adventure is sweet, not even a bit oldie!

But where's that hidden wisdom they promise me?
It seems to hide in a pot of cold tea.
Or laughing with friends over ice-cream cake,
In silly pursuits, is where I partake.

So I journey forward with pie in my hand,
The joy of the ride, I surely have planned.
Through laughter and crumbs, I boldly profess,
Life's quests are best when you don't have to stress.

Threads of Purpose

A sewing kit beckons with needles and thread,
I ponder if purpose includes what's been fed.
Half-finished projects lay strewn all about,
Like my thoughts on lasagna, they swim and they shout.

I stitched together a patchwork of dreams,
In colors so bright, they burst at the seams.
But my cat has decided it's fine to unwind,
With a flick of her paw, unravels my mind.

The fabric of life's an odd, quirky quilt,
With stitches of laughter and love that won't wilt.
There's beauty in chaos, I've heard it before,
Even if it means cleaning up off the floor.

So I'll wear my confusion, a hat that's askew,
For fashion's subjective and this much is true.
In each tangled thread, I'll find what I seek,
With humor and joy, this life's truly unique.

In the Labyrinth of Thought

Through mazes of musings, I wander and roam,
Tripping on ideas, I call them my home.
A squirrel darts past with a nut in its grip,
I ask it for guidance, it just takes a dip.

In corners of nonsense, I might find a clue,
Like socks in the dryer that once were a crew.
They argue what happened; each blames the other,
In the end, they just drift, like my thought-ways must flutter.

A signpost appears that says, "Take a left,"
Leading to cookies and a solid cleft.
But wait, there's a pitfall of misplaced keys,
I'll pause for a laugh at the absurdities.

At the end of this maze, I find the great door,
With scribbles of truths that can't be ignored.
In madness and mirth, I'll come back to play,
For wisdom is waiting in life's funny ballet.

Echoes of the Quiet Heart

In a land where socks go missing,
I ponder where my keys have been.
The fridge hums a tune so brimming,
While I snack and chat with unseen.

On Tuesdays, I find the lost remote,
Underneath the couch, it does float.
The cat gives me a knowing look,
As I hunt for things like a goofball crook.

My thoughts wander in the pantry's deep,
Where old spices sit and secrets keep.
Each jar whispers tales of yore,
Of pizzas and parties I can't ignore.

In the chaos of my jumbled mind,
Laughter leads me, a friend so kind.
With every giggle, I find the art,
Of enjoying the echoes of my heart.

The Compass of Lost Souls

My compass spins like a DJ's beat,
Leading to places I can't compete.
Last week it pointed to the fridge,
Where pizza dreams dance on the edge.

Every map I've drawn ends in a crumple,
Scribbled notes, my silent jumble.
X marks the spot, or so they say,
Yet I find myself in the neighbor's bay.

I ask a bird for directions near,
It flies away without a care.
With breadcrumbs and giggles, I start anew,
GPS? Nah! Just me and my shoe.

In the quest where I roam around,
Every laugh is a treasure found.
So I'll wander with light-hearted grace,
As the compass twirls in a silly chase.

Illumination in Shadows

In the depths where lost socks hide,
I trip over thoughts I can't abide.
The lamp flickers, hangs on a whim,
Illuminating my coffee's tiny rim.

Bathtubs echo with mystery moans,
While the dishwasher hums some tones.
Here in shadows, I crack a smile,
As the broom does a jig, oh, such style.

Under the bed, dust bunnies abound,
They chuckle softly, making no sound.
Each ghostly laugh dances in the night,
Bringing courage to my jesting fright.

In these alleys of whimsy and glee,
Laughter lights paths that can be seen.
So I skip through life with a jovial pride,
Trusting the shadows where joy can abide.

Navigating the Pathless Journey

Without a map and no GPS,
I wander in shorts, oh what a mess!
Chasing squirrels, I trip on my feet,
They snicker and scurry, oh what a feat!

Through tangled trails, I make my way,
With a sandwich tucked for a midday play.
Each step a giggle, each turn a tease,
As nature roars, I beg, "Please!"

Raccoons join me for a snack and cheer,
While I wonder if I'm heading here or there.
With stars in my eyes, I ask the moon,
"Which way to go? I should be back soon!"

So I stroll this path that's all misaligned,
With laughter and snacks, I'm genuinely blind.
In this jolly dance of pathless grace,
I find joy in not knowing my place.

The Alchemy of Lost Questions

In the fridge, I find my dreams,
Where leftovers fight for gleams.
Forgotten thoughts in Tupperware,
I ponder life with half a pear.

Like socks that vanish in the wash,
My deep thoughts slip and dash.
I ask my cat for life advice,
She just blinks, and rolls like dice.

Banana peels give wisdom true,
"Why rush?" they say, "Just have a chew."
Between the crumbs of yesterday,
I trip on truths that dance and sway.

I toss my dreams like paper planes,
They circle back through joy and pains.
In scattered laughter, I might find,
The gold that's hidden in my mind.

Stars that Guide Our Wanderings

Under a sky of cotton candy,
I navigate like a lost Andy.
Constellations shaped like pizzas float,
Remind me why I came by yacht.

With wishful eyes, I chase a star,
But bump my head on a nearby car.
Astronomy's a jester's game,
I laugh aloud; it's all the same.

My compass spins, it's rather rude,
A mood ring shows it's in a mood.
Galactic maps are printed wrong,
Yet through the chaos, I feel strong.

In cosmic cheese, I find my fate,
With every twinkle, I celebrate.
The universe whispers silly dreams,
In the absurd, I burst at seams.

Charting the Course of Inner Landscapes

Navigating thoughts like a bumpy road,
In my mind, a circus explodes.
Clowns in suits share wisdom blunt,
With every honk, they pull a stunt.

The trees are scribbled with my fears,
Each leaf a tale of laughter-cheers.
I chase my thoughts like popsicle sticks,
Bouncing ideas, doing tricks.

Maps made of chocolate lead me astray,
With every bite, I lose my way.
My brain's a maze of snack-filled quests,
In search of joy, I jest and jest.

A treasure chest of giggles bright,
In every corner, there's delight.
With every misstep, I cartwheel free,
In the playground of my mind, I see.

The Pulse of the Universe

The universe beats like a bass guitar,
With rhythms that take me near and far.
In a café, I sip on the stars,
Wishing for cosmic chocolate bars.

Each heartbeat hums a silly tune,
As aliens dance beneath the moon.
They juggle planets, throw confetti,
In this space, I feel all ready.

Galaxies giggle at my plight,
"Chill out, human! It's okay, right?"
Meteor showers in the shape of pies,
Fall from the sky, oh what a surprise!

In the rhythm of life, I groove and sway,
The pulse of the world leads me each day.
With humor nestled between the stars,
I chase the magic—forget my scars.

Nature's Silent Lessons

A squirrel grins with nuts in tow,
Teaching us to reap what we sow.
The trees whisper secrets from long ago,
While flowers dance in a sunlit glow.

A frog leaps high, wearing a crown,
Reminding us that we may fall down.
Yet still with a splash, he won't wear a frown,
In life's little puddles, don't drown in a gown.

The wind chuckles as it plays with leaves,
Not a care, as it teases the eaves.
Nature's jokes are surely the keys,
To laughter that flows like buzzing bees.

So next time you're lost in the daily grind,
Look at the antics the critters unwind.
In nature's comedy, wisdom you'll find,
Just keep an eye out, and love will be blind.

Beneath the Veil of Everyday

A coffee spill, so dark and wise,
Foreshadows mornings with sleepy sighs.
The toast jumps up, the butter flies,
Life's little surprises take us by size.

In crowded trains, the awkward stares,
Funny faces and mismatched pairs.
We all wear socks that show our cares,
As strangers giggle, nothing compares.

Elevator chats that fizzle and pop,
Share jokes with the walls, just don't stop!
From clumsy steps to the drop of a mop,
In mundane moments, we reach for the top.

So amidst the rush and daily schemes,
Look for laughter in life's little beams.
Behind every veil, the absurdity gleams,
It's the silly bits that fulfill the dreams.

Echoes of Unspoken Desires

In a cupboard, a cookie jar sings,
'Eat me now!' oh, the joy it brings.
But diets call like zealous kings,
While cravings dance with sugar wings.

A cat eyes a bird, both play their parts,
Staring contests pull at the hearts.
As laughter soars, reality departs,
Chasing whims, we outsmart the smarts.

A mailman slips on a runaway shoe,
Carrying dreams in a bag, it's true.
Postcards whisper where lovers flew,
And mishaps swirl like a playful brew.

In silence, we ponder the unneeded things,
As comedy wraps around life's little slings.
In each laugh, a new thought springs,
Echoes of desire shape the joy that clings.

Windows to the Eternal

A goldfish swims in circles grand,
Plotting worlds with a flick of a fin.
He dreams of races and castles of sand,
While children giggle, enjoying the whim.

A cat on the windowsill sips the sun,
Napping dreams of a great, grand chase.
Life with each purr, a playful pun,
While shadows dance in a furry embrace.

An old man in a hat gives a wink,
As pigeons plot their breadcrumb spree.
Life's a big joke, 'don't take a blink,'
While laughter rolls like tumbling debris.

So peer through the glass, let your heart roam,
In the oddities found, may we find our home.
Every chuckle and sigh, like a playful poem,
Are windows to treasures we proudly comb.

When Time Speaks in Riddles

Tick-tock, the clock's on a spree,
It laughs as it hides behind a tree.
With every second, it plays a prank,
I ponder my life; what do I thank?

A sock's lost here, the other's there,
A riddle wrapped in morning air.
Do I chase the light or hug the shade?
The laughs of time, a masquerade!

In shadows cast by hands of fate,
Mismatched shoes and a guessing gait.
What's wisdom's output, a legacy,
Or just a bad joke of history?

The more I think, the less I know,
Life's a game of peek-a-boo show.
With giggles that echo through the night,
I sum it up: Just enjoy the flight!

The Treasure Hidden in Plain Sight

A cookie jar marked 'do not touch',
But cookies beg, 'Oh, just one much?'
In cabinets where mischief stirs,
I find sweet treasures, disguised by blurs.

My friend says gold is where it's at,
But I found a cat snuggled in a hat.
His purring secrets fill the room,
Turns out, the real prize is the cat's zoom.

Maps show where X marks a spot,
But off the path, the fun is caught!
The laughter shared on streets unknown,
Yields more treasure than jewels alone.

So here's to those who overlook,
Life's mysteries written in storybook.
Finding joy in the giggles bright,
Is treasure found in plain sight.

The Colors of a Wandering Mind

A paintbrush dips in thoughts so wild,
Swirls of blue for the carefree child.
Green for envy, oh look, there's red,
As my own brain's circus unfolds, widespread.

Each hue whispers secrets to my soul,
The mundane sparks a vibrant goal.
Oh look! A polka-dotted thought,
Riding on waves of what I sought.

In every corner, colors collide,
Purple dreams where silliness resides.
The art of living, a funny spree,
What's serious? A laugh? Just let it be!

So splash your palette across the sky,
Let the colors dance and fly.
In this gallery of the mind,
Wandering is the best it's designed!

In Search of Sunlight Through the Canopy

Amidst the trees, I lost my way,
But the squirrels jest, 'Come out and play!'
With branches laughing overhead,
I trip on roots and doubt instead.

A sunbeam peeks through leafy green,
'Here I am!' says light—so keen!
But why does it hide behind a cloud?
Making me feel lost yet so proud.

A dance with shadows, a cheeky game,
Nature giggles, oh, it's to blame!
Each stumble, each plaid shirt snagged,
Adds to the hilarity as I lag.

Yet through the muck, I find my cheer,
The trees agree—adventure's near!
So laughter rings through wood and leaf,
Finding humor in the brief.

Reflections on a Calm Lake

In the lake I lose my face,
Fish swim by, a goofy grace.
Where's my watch? Oh, how absurd!
Just ducks quack, not wisdom's word.

Ripples laugh, a silly dance,
Hoping turtles take a chance.
What's the point of all this fun?
Oh look! There goes a ducky run.

Logs float by with stories old,
Hiding secrets, wise yet bold.
With every splash, I ponder deep,
Should I dive or take a leap?

As clouds tiptoe across the sky,
I muse on life while passers-by.
Oh, what a riddle, or a jest!
Maybe it's all a playful quest.

Traces of Truth in the Mist

In the fog, I lose my way,
Thoughts get lost in shades of gray.
Floating memories, hard to catch,
Like those socks my dog might snatch.

Raindrops giggle on my nose,
Is it wisdom, or just woes?
I trip over a mental block,
Was that a thought, or just a rock?

Voices whisper in the breeze,
What's the answer? Where's the cheese?
In this mist, it's hard to see,
But I swear that squirrel laughed at me.

So I dance between the trees,
Searching for my lost car keys.
In this haze, I find delight,
Muffled truths just out of sight.

The Longing in the Wind's Whisper

The wind calls softly, what's the score?
I listen close, it talks of lore.
Pine trees scribble secrets, sly,
But all I hear is, 'Where's my pie?'

The leaves chuckle, swirling down,
Am I a sage or just a clown?
Should I chase the breeze with glee,
Or sit and sip my herbal tea?

Old branches creak, a secret sigh,
Trees can gossip, oh me, oh my!
But the real truth, I still can't find,
Is it in nature, or in my mind?

So I twirl like dandelion fluff,
This pondering can be quite tough.
Yet, in laughter, I find my peace,
In silly thoughts, my joy won't cease.

Serendipity Beneath the Surface

Beneath the waves, a treasure waits,
Is it wisdom or fish on plates?
Mermaids giggle, weave a tale,
Waves of laughter, like a whale.

Coral castles, crabs that dance,
What if I took a silly chance?
Flippers flapping, "Join the fun!"
But oh, I can't swim, I just run.

Schooling fish with glasses on,
Debate if I'm just a con.
"Are you here for pearls or jest?"
Oh look, a floating, feathery vest!

So I bob along, quite absurd,
Pondering life, and feeling blurred.
In every dive, a giggle's brewed,
Serendipity often construed.

9 781805 662211